SHEPHERDS, WHY THIS JUBILEE?

JEFFREY R. HOLLAND

EAGLE GATE

IMAGE CREDITS

Harry Anderson: *Second Coming*, p. 43.

Robert Barrett: *No Room in the Inn*, p. 4; *Wise Man with Jesus*, p. 7; *Luke Writing the Christmas Story*, p. 29; *New Star Appeared*, p. 39; *Simeon and the Baby Jesus*, p. 56; *Flight into Egypt*, p. 69.

Simon Dewey: *Nativity*, pp. 1, 18-19; *The Resurrection*, p. 72.

Greg Olsen: *The Reason for the Season*, pp. 23, 25; *Simeon with the Christ Child*, pp. 52-53.

Del Parson: *Witness of the Birth*, pp. 34, 49, and front cover.

Liz Lemon Swindle: *She Shall Bring Forth a Son*, p. 14.

Quotations on pages 2-3 and 21 from *How the Grinch Stole Christmas!* by Dr. Seuss. TM & copyright © by Dr. Seuss Enterprises, L.P., 1957, renewed 1985. Reprinted by permission of Random House Children's Books, a division of Random House, Inc.

Eagle Gate is a registered trademark of Deseret Book Company.

Visit us at www.deseretbook.com

Library of Congress Cataloging-in-Publication Data
Holland, Jeffrey R., 1940-
    Shepherds, why this jubilee? / Jeffrey R. Holland.
      p. cm.
    ISBN 1-57345-863-5 (hardcover)
    1. Jesus Christ–Nativity. 2. Christmas.
BX8643.J4 H65 2000
242'.335–dc21
                                        00-056143

Printed in the United States of America
10 9 8 7 6 5 4 3 2 1   72082-6749

CONTENTS

MAYBE CHRISTMAS

DOESN'T COME

FROM A STORE

You will recall from Dr. Seuss's harrowing holiday story, *How the Grinch Stole Christmas!*, that this loathsome little man was determined to rob *Who*-ville of every holiday treat. In a nefarious scheme in which the Grinch dressed as Santa himself, he moved through *Who*-ville taking every package, tree, ornament, and stocking.

s he left the city with his sack full of stolen gifts, he chuckled in delight over the pain his actions would cause the people of *Who*-ville. He climbed to the top of a mountain where he anxiously waited to hear the sound of youthful anguish coming from the city below. He even cupped his hand to his ear in eager anticipation.

But what he heard instead were the joyful sounds of happy people celebrating Christmas. He was chagrined—and amazed. He couldn't imagine it, but Christmas had arrived in spite of him! Though the people of *Who*-ville had no trees to trim, no ornaments to enjoy, no packages to unwrap, they were having a wonderful Christmas anyway. It was more than the Grinch could fathom.

AND HE PUZZLED THREE HOURS, TILL HIS PUZZLER WAS SORE.

THEN THE GRINCH THOUGHT OF SOMETHING HE HADN'T BEFORE!

"MAYBE CHRISTMAS," HE THOUGHT, "DOESN'T COME FROM A STORE.

"MAYBE CHRISTMAS . . . PERHAPS . . . MEANS A LITTLE BIT MORE!"[1]

Part of the purpose for telling the real story of Christmas is to remind us that Christmas doesn't come from a store. Indeed, however delighted we feel about it, even as children, each year it "means a little bit more." And no matter how many times we read the biblical account of that evening in Bethlehem, we always come away with a thought— or two—we haven't had before.

There are so many lessons to be learned from the sacred account of Christ's birth that we hesitate to emphasize a few at the expense of all the others. Forgive me as I do just that.

3

"There was no room for them in the inn."

ne impression that has persisted with me over the years is that ~~this is a story~~—in profound paradox with our own times—~~of intense poverty.~~ I wonder if Luke did not have some special meaning when he wrote not that "there was no room in the inn" but specifically that ~~"there was no room for them in the inn."~~ (LUKE 2:7; EMPHASIS ADDED.) We cannot be certain, but it is my guess that money could talk in those days as well as in our own. I think if Joseph and Mary had been people of influence or means, they would have found lodging even at that busy time of year.

I have also wondered if the Joseph Smith Translation was suggesting they ~~did not know the "right people"~~ in saying, ~~"There was none to give room for them in the inns."~~ (JST LUKE 2:7.)

We cannot be certain what the historian intended, but we do know these two were desperately poor. At the purification offering which the parents made after the child's birth, two turtledoves were substituted for the required lamb, a substitution the Lord had allowed in the law of Moses to ease the burden of the truly impoverished. (LEVITICUS 12:8.)

The wise men did come later bearing gifts, adding some splendor and wealth to this occasion, but it is important to note that they came from a distance, probably ancient Persia, a trip of several hundred miles at the very least. Unless they started long before the star appeared, it is highly unlikely that they arrived on the night of the Babe's birth. Indeed, Matthew records that when they came, Jesus was a "young child" and the family was living in a "house." (MATTHEW 2:11.)

Perhaps this provides an important distinction we should remember in our own holiday season. Maybe the purchasing and the making and the wrapping and the decorating—those delightfully generous and important expressions of our love at

The wise men did come
later bearing gifts . . .

Christmas—should be separated slightly from the more quiet, personal moments when we consider the meaning of the Baby (and his birth) who prompts the giving of such gifts.

s happens so often if we are not careful, the symbols can overwhelm the symbolized. In modern times there is always a risk that the manger so central to the Christmas story will be torn down to make way for a discount store featuring specials on a host of Christmas "bargains."

I do not feel—or mean to sound—like a modern-day Scrooge. Gold, frankincense, and myrrh were humbly given and appreciatively received, and so gifts from the heart should be given every year and always.

But for that very reason, I, like you, need to remember the very plain scene, even the poverty, of a night devoid of tinsel or wrapping or goods of this world. Only when we see that single, sacred, unadorned object of our devotion, the Babe of Bethlehem, and understand his mission to save all mankind will we know why "'tis the season to be jolly" and why the giving of gifts is so appropriate— our "little" gifts serving as loving, selfless reminders of his loving, selfless, majestic, redeeming gift.

As a father I have thought often of Joseph, that strong, silent, almost unknown man who must have been more worthy than any other mortal man to be the guiding foster father of the living Son of God. It was Joseph, selected from among all men, who would teach Jesus to work. It was Joseph who taught him the books of the law. It was Joseph who, in the seclusion of the shop, helped him begin to understand who he was and ultimately what he was to become.

I was a student at Brigham Young University just finishing my first year of graduate work when our first child, a son, was born. We were very poor, though not so poor as Joseph and Mary. My wife and I were both going to school, both holding jobs, and in addition worked as head residents in an off-campus apartment complex to help defray our rent. We drove a little Volkswagen which always had a half-dead battery because we couldn't afford a new one (Volkswagen or battery).

evertheless, when I realized that our own night of nights was coming, I believe I would have done any honorable thing in this world, and mortgaged any future I had, to make sure my wife had the clean sheets, the sterile utensils, the attentive nurses, and the skilled doctors who brought forth our firstborn son. If she or that child had needed special care at the Mayo Clinic, I believe I would have ransomed my very life to get it.

I compare those feelings (which I have had with each succeeding child) with what Joseph must have felt as he moved through the streets of a city not his own, with not a friend or kinsman in sight, nor anyone willing to extend a helping hand. In these very last and most painful hours of her "confinement," Mary had ridden or walked approximately one hundred miles from Nazareth in Galilee to Bethlehem in Judea. Surely Joseph must have wept at her silent courage. Now, alone and unnoticed, they had to descend from human company to a stable, a grotto full of animals, there to bring forth the Son of God.

 wonder what emotions Joseph might have had as he cleared away the dung and debris. I wonder if he felt the sting of tears as he hurriedly tried to find the cleanest straw and hold the animals back. I wonder if he wondered: "Could there be a more unhealthy, a more disease-ridden, a more despicable circumstance in which a child could be born? Is this a place fit for a king? Should the mother of the Son of God be asked to enter the valley of the shadow of death in such a foul and unfamiliar place as this? Is it wrong to wish her some comfort? Is it right He should be born here?"

ut I am certain Joseph did not mutter and Mary did not wail. They knew a great deal, had the help of the Holy Spirit, and did the best they could.

Perhaps these parents knew even then that in the beginning of his mortal life, as well as in the end, this baby son born to them would have to descend beneath every human pain and disappointment. He would do so, at least in part, to help those who also felt they had been born without advantage.

I have thought of Mary, too, this most favored mortal woman in the history of the world, who as a mere child received an angel who uttered to her those words that would change the course not only of her own life but also that of all human history: "HAIL, THOU VIRGIN, WHO ART HIGHLY FAVORED OF THE LORD. THE LORD IS WITH THEE; FOR THOU ART CHOSEN AND BLESSED AMONG WOMEN." (JST LUKE 1:28.) The nature of her spirit and the depth of her preparation were revealed in a response that shows

both innocence and maturity: "BEHOLD THE HAND-
MAID OF THE LORD; BE IT UNTO ME ACCORDING TO
THY WORD." (LUKE 1:38.)

It is here I stumble, here that I grasp for the feelings a mother has when she knows she has conceived
a living soul, feels life quicken and grow within her
womb, and carries a child to delivery. At such times
fathers stand aside and watch, but mothers feel and
never forget. Again, I've thought of Luke's careful
phrasing about that holy night in Bethlehem:

THE DAYS WERE ACCOMPLISHED THAT *SHE* . . .
BROUGHT FORTH *HER* FIRSTBORN SON, AND
[*SHE*] WRAPPED HIM IN SWADDLING CLOTHES,
AND [*SHE*] LAID HIM IN A MANGER. (LUKE 2:6–7;
EMPHASIS ADDED.)

Those brief pronouns trumpet in our ears that,
second only to the child himself, Mary is the chiefest
figure here, the regal queen, mother of mothers—
holding center stage in this grandest of all dramatic

" . . . she brought forth
her firstborn son"

moments. And those same pronouns also trumpet that, save for her beloved husband, she was very much alone.

have wondered if this young woman, something of a child herself, here bearing her first baby, might have wished her mother, or an aunt, or her sister, or her friend to be near her through the labor. Surely the birth of such a son as this should have commanded the aid and attention of every midwife in Judea. We all might wish that someone could have held her hand, cooled her brow, and when the ordeal was over, given her rest in crisp, cool linen.

But it was not to be so. With only Joseph's inexperienced assistance, she herself brought forth her firstborn son, wrapped him in the little clothes she had knowingly brought on her journey, and perhaps laid him on a pillow of hay.

Then, on both sides of the veil, a heavenly host broke into song. "GLORY TO GOD IN THE HIGHEST," they sang. "PEACE UPON EARTH AMONG MEN OF GOODWILL." (LUKE 2:14, PHILLIPS TRANSLATION.) But except for heavenly witnesses, these three were alone: Joseph, Mary, and the baby to be named Jesus.

t this focal point of all human history, a point illuminated by a new star in the heavens revealed for just such a purpose, probably no other mortal watched— none but a poor young carpenter, a beautiful virgin mother, and silent stabled animals who had not the power to utter the sacredness they had seen.

Shepherds would soon arrive and, later, wise men from the East. Later yet the memory of that night would allow for Santa Claus and Frosty and Rudolph—all of whom would add to our delight. But first and forever there was just a little family, without toys or trees or tinsel. With a baby—that's how Christmas began.

"Peace upon

earth among

men of

goodwill."

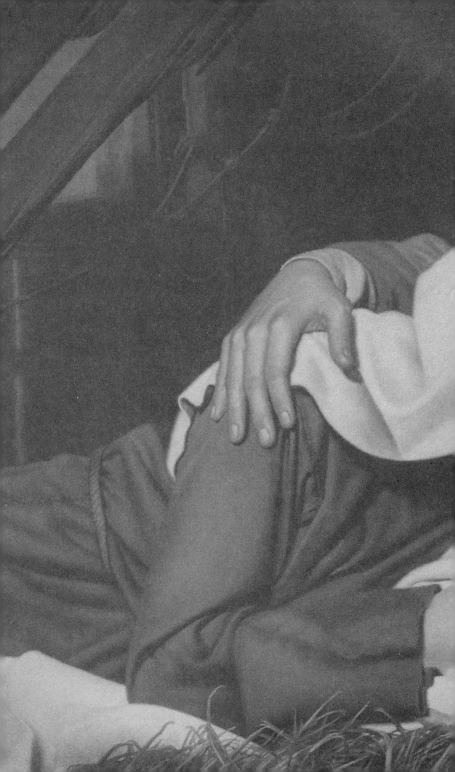

It is for this baby that we shout in chorus:

Hark! the herald angels sing
Glory to the newborn King!
. . . Mild he lays his glory by,
Born that man no more may die;
Born to raise the sons of earth,
Born to give them second birth.[2]

Perhaps recalling the circumstances of that gift, of his birth, of his own childhood, perhaps remembering that purity and faith and genuine humility will be required of every celestial soul, Jesus must have said many times as he looked into the little eyes that loved him (eyes that always best saw what and who he really was), "EXCEPT YE BE CONVERTED, AND BECOME AS LITTLE CHILDREN, YE SHALL NOT ENTER INTO THE KINGDOM OF HEAVEN." (MATTHEW 18:3.)

Christmas, then, is for children—of all ages. I suppose that is why my favorite Christmas carol is a child's song. I sing it with more emotion than any other:

Away in a manger,

no crib for his bed,

The little Lord Jesus

laid down his sweet head. . . .

I love thee, Lord Jesus;

look down from the sky

And stay by my cradle

till morning is nigh.

Be near me, Lord Jesus;

I ask thee to stay

Close by me forever,

and love me, I pray.

Bless all the dear children

in thy tender care,

And fit us for heaven

to live with thee there. [3]

"Then the Grinch thought of something he hadn't before! 'Maybe Christmas,' he thought, 'doesn't come from a store.'"

NOTES

1. DR. SEUSS, *HOW THE GRINCH STOLE CHRISTMAS!*, NEW YORK: RANDOM HOUSE, 1957.
2. "HARK! THE HERALD ANGELS SING," *HYMNS* (SALT LAKE CITY: THE CHURCH OF JESUS CHRIST OF LATTER-DAY SAINTS, 1985), NO. 209.
3. "AWAY IN A MANGER," *HYMNS*, NO. 206.

AND SAINTS AND

ANGELS SING

Some things just go with Christmas. Whether we call these "the spirit of the season" or "memories of youth" or simply "holiday traditions," we all know what invokes the spirit of Christmas for us. Whatever our personal favorite traditions are, one above all others seems to turn our hearts joyfully to the Savior of the world and the real meaning of his birth. It is not the shopping, though that can be fun if it remains reasonable and modest. It is not the

SHEPHERDS, WHY THIS JUBILEE?

decorations, though they are certainly signs that Christmas is upon us. And it is not the food that seems to appear with every ring of the doorbell! No, I think the most universal indication that the holiday season is here is the music—the caroling, the hymns, those favorites we sing at home, hear over the radio, maybe even catch in stores or in the street, and find especially inspiring at Church meetings.

I don't know how it is at your house, but we don't do much decorating until a week or two into December. As for shopping, I leave that until *late* December. Pat bakes the children's—and now the grandchildren's—favorite holiday recipes, though that, too, is pretty much a December experience. But the hymns and carols! Our daughter would start on them sometime in early October! "Just getting ready," she would say. "You can't get the piano warmed up too early for Christmas," she would declare, and then roll into another chorus of "Joy to the World." Well, now that she and her brothers are

. . . they are certainly signs that Christmas is upon us.

grown, married, and having little nativities of their own, we miss that music and think back on it with special delight—one of those ingredients we will cherish forever in our Christmas memories. So as December comes, Pat and I make sure the carols are still in our home—she on the piano, I on the radio, tape deck, and CD player. I am, after all, multi-musical.

uilding upon the spirit of love and generosity so prevalent in this festive season, I am convinced it is the hymns and carols that convey the real message of Christmas most consistently during the holidays. Only the scriptures themselves (which often provide the text for our Christmas hymns), give more direct doctrine regarding the birth of the Savior and its meaning for mankind. Perhaps it is some natural—no, divine—impulse that when we think of Jesus' birth, life, and love, of his sacrifice, his atonement, and resurrection—we have to sing! Every one of us! Even those of us who can't carry a tune at all.

Somehow that doesn't matter at Christmas. Everyone sings, and well we should. The Lord has said his soul (Do we think often enough about *God's* soul and what pleases it?) "DELIGHTETH IN THE SONG OF THE HEART; YEA, THE SONG OF THE RIGHTEOUS IS A PRAYER UNTO ME." (D&C 25:12.)

I don't know whether you have thought of the Christmas hymns and carols as Christmas prayers, but they are. They are pleasing to the soul of the Father. Maybe it is evidence to him that we are grateful for his ultimate Christmas gift to us—the Babe of Bethlehem himself—and that we have not forgotten from whom and by whom that gift came. Even a little out of tune or slightly off-key, the Christmas hymn of the righteous is a prayer unto God. Through good times and bad, even in the sorrow and difficulty that occasionally accompany Christmas for some, the fact of the matter is that Christ's birth has brought "joy to the world, [for] the Lord [has] come. . . . Let ev'ry heart prepare him room, and Saints and angels sing."[1]

s one way to retell the Christmas story may we gather our families around us and, having read again the Christmas story in the second chapter of Luke, sing together—or at least share the text of—the traditional hymns and carols of Christmas that teach us so much about this grand event.

The scriptures begin the Christmas story by explaining that as a result of Roman decree, Joseph and Mary were to leave Nazareth and go to their "own city" to pay a census tax. Little did the pagan Augustus know he was helping to fulfill prophecy when he required Joseph and Mary to pay their tax at precisely the time Mary was "great with child" (LUKE 2:5) and about to deliver her holy son. Roman law would have allowed this young couple to stay in Nazareth, the place of their residence, to pay their tax and be counted in the enrollment. However, Jewish tradition held that such a registration must be undertaken in the ancestral homes of the respective families. Undoubtedly Joseph and Mary

"A Saviour, which is Christ the Lord," had been born in a nearby stable.

knew they were going to Bethlehem for far more
spiritual reasons than either Roman governors or
Jewish rabbis understood.

In the Christmas hymn, "While Shepherds
Watched Their Flocks," the angels announced to
the shepherds:

> *"To you, in David's town this day,*
> *Is born of David's line*
> *The Savior who is Christ the Lord,*
> *And this shall be the sign:*
> *The heav'nly Babe you there shall find*
> *To human view displayed,*
> *All meanly wrapped in swathing bands,*
> *And in a manger laid."*[2]

"David's town" and "David's line" are, of course,
crucially important to this story. Although there
were differences of opinion even then regarding the
specific circumstances that were to accompany the

arrival of the Messiah, certain essentials were beyond question. Certainly the Messiah was to be born in a royal lineage that included Abraham, Judah, and David. As part of that Davidic heritage, the Messiah would be born in Bethlehem, "Royal David's City."[3]

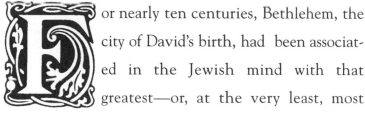

or nearly ten centuries, Bethlehem, the city of David's birth, had been associated in the Jewish mind with that greatest—or, at the very least, most popular—of all of Israel's kings. It was at Bethlehem that the prophet Samuel anointed David to be king. (1 SAMUEL 16:1, 4, 13.) Later the prophet Micah, pointing toward the advent of Christ, the rightful heir of David's crown, prophesied,

"BUT THOU, BETH-LEHEM EPHRATAH, THOUGH THOU BE LITTLE AMONG THE THOUSANDS OF JUDAH, YET OUT OF THEE SHALL HE COME FORTH UNTO ME THAT IS TO BE RULER IN ISRAEL; WHOSE GOINGS FORTH HAVE BEEN FROM OF OLD, FROM EVERLASTING." (MICAH 5:2.)

wo genealogical accounts in the scriptures document this ~~royal Davidic heritage, a gift Jesus received not only from his foster father Joseph but also from his mother Mary~~. It is generally conceded that Matthew's account (MATTHEW 1:1–17) is that of the royal lineage, establishing the order of sequence among legal successors to David's throne. Traditionally this has been seen as Joseph's line. This means that had Judea been a free and independent nation ruled by her true sovereign, Joseph, the carpenter from Galilee, would have been its king. His lawful (though, in this very special case, not literal) successor to the throne would have been Jesus of Nazareth, rightfully "the King of the Jews."

On the other hand, Luke's genealogical record (LUKE 3:23–38) is a personal pedigree, made without regard for the legal line of succession to the throne. This record is usually considered to be the pedigree for Mary, who certainly understood her royal role in this birth. When the angel told Mary of the birth of

Christ, he said, "The Lord God shall give him the throne of his father David." If Joseph, her betrothed, had alone been descended from David, Mary would have answered, "I am not yet married to Joseph," but she answered, "I am an unmarried woman." This implies the meaning—"If I were married, since I am descended from David, I could infuse my royal blood into a son, but how can I have a royal son while I am a virgin?"[4]

This is just one of the doctrines that is taught more clearly in the hymns and carols of Christmas than it is in any other holiday tradition. We sing, "Joy to the world, the Lord is come; Let earth receive her King!"[5] And "Come to Bethlehem and see him whose birth the angels sing; Come, adore on bended knee Christ the Lord, the newborn King."[6] And again, "Oh, come, all ye faithful, joyful and triumphant! Oh, come ye, oh, come ye to Bethlehem. Come and behold him, born the King of angels; Oh, come, let us adore him . . . Christ, the Lord."[7]

hat reference to angels in the scriptures and in the carols reminds us how important this event was on the other side of the veil. The angel Gabriel had already come to Zacharias announcing the conception and future birth of Zacharias' and Elizabeth's son, John, later to be known as the Baptist. (LUKE 1:5–25.) That same Gabriel then came to Mary while she was yet unmarried and announced to her the miracle that was to happen: her conceiving and bearing Jesus, the Son of the living God. (LUKE 1:26–38.)

With such conspicuous involvement from those attending to matters in heaven, it is little wonder that an angel appeared to the shepherds in the fields adjacent to Bethlehem, announcing to them that "a Saviour, which is Christ the Lord," had been born in a nearby stable. (LUKE 2:8–12.) At that moment a multitude of angels, a heaven full of angels, appeared, singing and praising God for the glory that was rightfully his and the promise that such a gift was to bring to the earth. Certainly we give thanks that then and now such an event did not go unnoticed in heaven, that "while mortals sleep, the angels keep their watch of wond'ring love."[8]

As important as angels are in our theology and as often as they have appeared to holy men and women through the ages, there had never been an angelic manifestation like this in all the world's history.

Angels we have heard on high
Sweetly singing o'er the plains,
And the mountains in reply
Echoing their joyous strains.[9]

Sing, choirs of angels,
Sing in exultation;
Sing, all ye citizens of heav'n above![10]

Surely the world did "in solemn stillness lay to hear the angels sing."[11]

Even "fields and floods, rocks, hills, and plains" felt to "repeat the sounding joy" of that moment.[12] This helps some of us summon our courage to join in the singing, even if we do not have angelic voices. Surely we can do as well as the rocks and the hills! And just in case we need urging, the refrain of another hymn goes: "And *Saints* and angels sing, and *Saints* and angels sing, and *Saints, and Saints* and angels sing."[13] I suspect that chorus is intentional in its emphasis on "and Saints." Clearly the angels don't need as much coaxing—or coaching—as we do.

ther elements of the beautiful Christmas story are touched upon in the hymns and carols. There was a star positioned and specially lighted in the heavens for this night of nights. (MATTHEW 2:2.) We do not know which star that was nor from whence it came nor how its light focused so directly on Bethlehem, but the Book of Mormon as well as the New Testament make it clear that such a light, a "new star," did appear. Indeed, the Book of

Mormon prophecy was that there would be "great lights [plural] in heaven, insomuch that in the night before he cometh there shall be no darkness [on the western continent], insomuch that it shall appear unto man as if it was day." (HELAMAN 14:3.) That prophecy was fulfilled in every detail. (SEE 3 NEPHI 1:15, 19–21.)

With wond'ring awe the wise men saw
The star in heaven springing,
And with delight, in peaceful night,
They heard the angels singing:

. . . By light of star they traveled far
To seek the lowly manger,
A humble bed wherein was laid
The wondrous little Stranger.

. . . The heav'nly star its rays afar
On ev'ry land is throwing,
And shall not cease till holy peace
In all the earth is growing.

Hosanna, hosanna,
hosanna to his name![14]

There would be "great lights in heaven . . ."

The hymns and carols also capture the simple splendor, even the meekness and poverty of the Savior's birth. Of this experience, we sing:

> *Once in royal David's city*
> *Stood a lowly cattle shed, . . .*
> *And his shelter was a stable,*
> *And his cradle was a stall;*
> *With the poor, and mean, and lowly,*
> *Lived on earth our Savior holy.*[15]

It would certainly seem the Son of God himself, the true King of kings, might have had more splendor surrounding him than this, but his mission was to everyone, including the disadvantaged, the weary, the sick, the poor. His life would begin as it would be lived—without any show of this world's goods, no home for his birth and a borrowed tomb at his death. We would say of his nativity what Jesus said of his life, "THE FOXES HAVE HOLES, AND THE BIRDS OF THE AIR HAVE NESTS; BUT THE SON OF MAN HATH NOT WHERE TO LAY HIS HEAD." (MATTHEW 8:20.)

"The heav'nly star

its rays afar

On ev'ry land

is throwing,

And shall not cease

till holy peace

In all the earth

is growing."

Surely this scene of poverty and plainness should have a place in our hearts in such a season of gift giving and material abundance. In some sad or lonely circumstances we might not have toys or trinkets, but we will *always* have Christmas! The best part—the central and eternal part—of this event was meant to be pure, simple, and unadorned.

inally, what may be most glorious about the hymns' celebration of Christ's advent is not only their telling of that first Christmas story but also their promise of a later one. This is a theme that runs through the carols and which may be lost in the season if we are not listening for it. Along with the joy of Christmas past is the anticipation of Christ's triumphant return and what will be made known by the angels again.

Indeed those angels are singing even now if we will but hear them:

Along with the joy
of Christmas past is the
anticipation of Christ's
triumphant return.

Still thru the cloven skies they come
With peaceful wings unfurled,
And still their heav'nly music floats
O'er all the weary world.
Above its sad and lowly plains
They bend on hov'ring wing,
And ever o'er its babel sounds
The blessed angels sing.

For lo! the days are hast'ning on,
By prophets seen of old,
When with the ever circling years
Shall come the time foretold,
When the new heav'n and earth shall own
The Prince of Peace their King,
And the whole world send back the song
Which now the angels sing.[16]

[Someday] . . . our eyes at last shall see him,
Through his own redeeming love;
For that child so dear and gentle
Is our Lord in heav'n above.[17]

n all of our celebration I pray that we will see "love's pure light," those "radiant beams" from his holy face. I pray that we will always see in him "the dawn of redeeming grace."[18] I am eternally grateful that in him and by him, we have genuine hope for peace in this world and eternal life in the world to come.

Mild he lays his glory by,
born that man no more may die;
Born to raise the sons of earth,
born to give them second birth.[19]

ecause of him we have the assurance that through his atonement and our repentance "no more will sin and sorrow grow, nor thorns infest the ground; he'll come and make the blessings flow far as the curse was found."[20]

How silently, how silently
The wondrous gift is giv'n!
So God imparts to human hearts
The blessings of his heav'n.
No ear may hear his coming;
But in this world of sin,
Where meek souls will receive him, still
The dear Christ enters in.[21]

"Shepherds, why this jubilee?"[22] We know why—
because it is Christmas! Joy and laughter, love and
family, friends and hope and salvation. That is why
this jubilee.

For all of this and more, we join in the hymns and
carols of the season. We take our places in the chorus
of all mankind, singing:

Lord, with the angels

      we too would rejoice;

Help us to sing

      with the heart and voice. . . .

Hasten the time when,

      from ev'ry clime,

Men shall unite

      in the strains sublime:

Glory to God,

      Glory to God,

Glory to God

      in the highest;

Peace on earth,

      goodwill to men;

Peace on earth,

      goodwill to men![23]

NOTES

1. "JOY TO THE WORLD," *HYMNS*, NO. 201.
2. "WHILE SHEPHERDS WATCHED THEIR FLOCKS," *HYMNS*, NO. 211.
3. "ONCE IN ROYAL DAVID'S CITY," *HYMNS*, NO. 205.
4. PARAPHRASED FROM CANON GIRDLESTONE, AS QUOTED IN JAMES E. TALMAGE, *JESUS THE CHRIST* (SALT LAKE CITY: DESERET BOOK COMPANY, 1962), P. 85.
5. *HYMNS*, NO. 201.
6. "ANGELS WE HAVE HEARD ON HIGH," *HYMNS*, NO. 203.
7. "OH, COME, ALL YE FAITHFUL," *HYMNS*, NO. 202.
8. "O LITTLE TOWN OF BETHLEHEM," *HYMNS*, NO. 208.
9. *HYMNS*, NO. 203.
10. *HYMNS*, NO. 202.
11. "IT CAME UPON A MIDNIGHT CLEAR," *HYMNS*, NO. 207.
12. *HYMNS*, NO. 201.
13. IBID.; EMPHASIS ADDED.
14. "WITH WONDERING AWE," *HYMNS*, NO. 210.
15. *HYMNS*, NO. 205.
16. *HYMNS*, NO. 207.
17. *HYMNS*, NO. 205.
18. "SILENT NIGHT," *HYMNS*, NO. 204.
19. "HARK! THE HERALD ANGELS SING," *HYMNS*, NO. 209.
20. *HYMNS*, NO. 201.
21. *HYMNS*, NO. 208.
22. *HYMNS*, NO. 203.
23. "FAR, FAR AWAY ON JUDEA'S PLAINS," *HYMNS*, NO. 212; EMPHASIS ADDED.

CHRISTMAS

COMFORT

The second chapter of Luke provides the text for many of the great stories of Christmas. My text is taken from those sacred verses, but the passage I have in mind is not a verse we often hear at this happy season of the year. Nevertheless, I believe it is at the heart of the Christmas message.

 speak of a beautiful moment, approximately forty days after Mary's delivery of the child, when she and Joseph took the baby named Jesus to the temple, where the infant was to be presented unto the Lord. It was desirable for all children to be so presented in the temple, but in the Israelite tradition it was of particular importance to present the firstborn son, a rite stemming from the miraculous days of salvation in Egypt when the firstborn of the Israelite families were spared destruction. In memorial all firstborn sons were thereafter dedicated to the service of the Lord, including Levitical service in the temple. It was not practical for every firstborn son to be presented in the temple, let alone to render service there; nevertheless the eldest son in a family was still claimed as the Lord's own in a special way and had to be formally exempted from his requirement by the paying of an offering of redemption.

It is here that we realize just how poor Joseph

and Mary were. The standard offering on behalf of such a child was a yearling lamb and a pigeon or turtledove. But in cases of severe poverty the law of Moses allowed the substitution of a second dove in place of the more expensive lamb. Mary and Joseph presented their son to his true Father that day with an offering of two turtledoves. This young couple, and this son who would save us, all knew what it was like to face economic privation at Christmastime.

As they made their way toward the temple that day, the Holy Spirit was resting upon a beloved elderly man named Simeon, one whom the scriptures describe as "just and devout." It was revealed to this gentle and venerable man that he would not die before seeing the Messiah—"the Lord's Christ," as Luke phrases it. The Spirit then led him to the temple, where he saw a young carpenter and his even younger wife enter the sanctuary with a newborn babe cradled in his mother's arms.

imeon, who had waited all his life for "the consolation of Israel," took that consolation in his arms, praised God, and said:

LORD, NOW LETTEST THOU THY SERVANT DEPART IN PEACE, ACCORDING TO THY WORD:

FOR MINE EYES HAVE SEEN THY SALVATION,

WHICH THOU HAST PREPARED BEFORE THE FACE OF ALL PEOPLE;

A LIGHT TO LIGHTEN THE GENTILES, AND THE GLORY OF THY PEOPLE ISRAEL.

AND JOSEPH AND HIS MOTHER MARVELLED AT THOSE THINGS WHICH WERE SPOKEN OF HIM.

AND SIMEON BLESSED THEM, AND SAID UNTO MARY HIS MOTHER, BEHOLD, THIS CHILD IS SET FOR THE FALL AND RISING AGAIN OF MANY IN ISRAEL; AND FOR A SIGN WHICH SHALL BE SPOKEN AGAINST;

(YEA, A SWORD SHALL PIERCE THROUGH THY OWN SOUL ALSO,) THAT THE THOUGHTS OF MANY HEARTS MAY BE REVEALED. (LUKE 2:29–35.)

here is a profound Christmas message in the one this dear old man gave to sweet and pure Mary in that first Christmas season. He was joyously happy. He had lived to see the Son of God be born. He had held the child in his very arms. He could now die the happiest man in all of Jerusalem, maybe in all the world. But his joy was not of the superficial kind. It was not without its testing and trying. In that sense it didn't have much to do with toys or trinkets or tinsel, though these have their Christmas place. No, his joy had something to do with "the fall and rising again of many in Israel," and with this child's life—or at least his death—which would be like a sword piercing through his beloved mother's soul. We might well ask, "Was such an ominous warning, such a fateful prophecy, appropriate in this season of joy? Surely such was untimely, even unseemly, at that moment—when the Son of God was so young and tender and safe, and his mother so thrilled with his birth and his beauty?"

Our answer is, yes, it was appropriate and important. I submit that unless we see all the meaning

"*Behold, this child is set for the fall and rising again . . .*"

and joy of Christmas the way old Simeon saw it all (and in a sense forced Joseph and Mary to see it)—the whole of Christ's life, the profound mission, the end as well as the beginning—then Christmas will be just another day off work, with food and fun and football for many and a measure of personal loneliness and family sorrow for others. The true meaning, the unique and lasting and joyous meaning of the birth of this baby, would be in the life he would lead and especially in his death, in his triumphant atoning sacrifice (remember why Joseph and Mary were in the temple), and in his prison-bursting resurrection.

It is the life at the other end of the manger scene that gives this moment of nativity in Bethlehem its ultimate meaning. Special as this child was and divine as was his conception, without that day of salvation wherein he would gain an everlasting victory over death and hell on behalf of every man, woman, and child who would ever be born—until that day should come—this baby's life and mission would not be complete. Worse yet, without that triumphant atonement and resurrection he might have been remembered only as one born in abject poverty, scorned in his own native village, and tortured to death by a ruthless Roman regime that knew everything about torture and death.

ut wise old Simeon understood all of this—that the birth was ultimately for the death—and it thrilled his soul that salvation was come. Thus Christmas was sobering as well as sweet for him, and so too will most Christmases be for us. Lying among those gifts of gold, frankincense, and myrrh were also a crown of thorns, a makeshift royal robe, and a Roman spear.

I do not want this to be an unhappy message—indeed, I intend it to be a supremely joyful message, a message of special comfort. But to make it that I must speak of Christmases (and many other days in our individual and collective lives) that for whatever reason may not be very happy or seem to be "the season to be jolly."

or many people in many places this may not be an entirely happy Christmas, one not filled with complete joy because of the circumstances facing a spouse or a friend, a child or a grandchild. Or perhaps that was the case another Christmas in another year, but one which brings a painful annual memory to us yet. Or (and may heaven bless us that this not be so) perhaps this may be the case some future Christmas when, unexpectedly and undeservedly, something goes terribly wrong, when there is some public or very personal tragedy in which it may seem, at least for a time, that "hate is strong and mocks the song of peace on earth, good will to men."[1]

By way of illustration let me share a few examples that I pray are not too painful or too personal for anyone who reads this. I recall that some years ago, in the very heart of the holiday season, a fire broke out on a conveyor belt five thousand feet into the Wilberg Mine near Orangeville in Emery

County, Utah. The story gripped the entire state and drew national attention. One man miraculously escaped, but all twenty-seven of the others had finally been found or declared dead by Sunday, December 23—two days before Christmas. On Monday, December 24, an article in the *Deseret News* began: "[Today] in church, watching his mother sob, Chris Pugliese knew that this Christmastime is [going to be] different. His mother, Kathy, lost no one in the Wilberg Mine fire, but she, like others, feels the pain of those who did. Chris may not quite understand that the sadness that dampened his family's Christmas destroyed the holiday joy of twenty-seven other families. Those families may never again celebrate Christmas without recalling the death of a father, son, daughter or brother."

More recently a tragedy struck even a little closer to our family. Exactly one week before Christmas in 1994—a Sunday morning—a freak accident on

Highway 128 nine miles northeast of Moab plunged four teenagers to their deaths in the frigid water of the Colorado River. They were magnificent young people by every standard—a student body president and valedictorian, two Eagle Scouts, a Laurel class president—traveling that morning to sing at a missionary friend's homecoming in nearby Castle Valley. Two of the four were brothers, Joseph and Gary Welling, exemplary sons of our childhood friend and twenty-year St. George schoolmate, Elaine Fawson Welling. This Christmas won't be as difficult for the Welling and Stewart and Adair families as that year, but it will be difficult. It will reopen a deep wound, and every Christmas for the rest of their lives will undoubtedly carry some echo of that pain and those family memories.

May I be even a bit more personal and in conclusion leave you with something more cheerful than all of this has been so far.

n the evening of December 23, 1976, my father underwent surgery to relieve the effect of osteoarthritis in the vertebrae of his back. The surgery was successful, but near the conclusion of it he suffered a major heart attack. Eight hours later he suffered another one. From those two attacks he sustained massive damage to a heart that was already defective from an illness suffered in his youth. By the time we finally got to see him, wired and tubed and gray and unconscious, it was mid-morning on December 24, Christmas Eve. "Magnificent timing," I muttered to no one in particular.

Pat and I stayed at his side all day, as much for my mother's sake as for my father's. He was not going to live, and at age sixty she had never had to confront that possibility in their entire married life. As evening came along, we took her to our home. She needed calming, and our three little children deserved some kind of Christmas Eve. Pat has created a wonderful world of holiday traditions in our family, and we tried to do the Christmas Eve portion of those, but it was a pretty joyless exercise. We tried to laugh and sing, but all that these children understood was that their grandmother was crying, their dad was very sad, and their grandfather was somewhere alone in a hospital, not free for the Christmas visit that had been planned. After hanging just a few of their mother's annual Christmas Eve gingerbread men, they uncharacteristically suggested that perhaps they should just go to bed a little early this year, reassuring everyone that this was their choice and something they really wanted to do. You can imagine how convincing they sounded. About as convincing as our caroling had been.

 gave my mother a blessing and convinced her to try to get some sleep. I stayed with Pat for a while, putting out a Christmas gift or two; then I told her to hold the family together—as she has done all of our married life—and I was going back to the hospital. There was obviously nothing I could do there.

She knew it and I knew it, but she also knew it was my Santa Claus who was lying alone with all those tubes, IVs, and monitors, and she said not a word to try to get me to remain.

At the hospital I sat and walked and read and walked and looked in on Dad and walked. He would not, in fact, recover from all this. I suppose everyone knew that, but the nursing staff were kind to me and gave me free access to him and to the entire hospital. A couple of the nurses wore Santa Claus hats, and all the nursing stations were decorated for the season. During the course of the evening I think I checked them all out, and sure enough, on every floor and in every wing it was Christmas.

You will forgive me if I admit that somewhere in the early hours of the morning I was feeling pretty sorry for myself. "Why does it have to be like this?" I thought. "Why does it have to be on Christmas?" Of all the times to lose your dad, did it have to be the time when dads are the greatest guys in the world and gifts for little boys somehow appear that, in later years, would be recognized to be well beyond the meager Holland budget? Lying under that oxygen tent was the most generous man I have ever known, a Kris Kringle to end all Kris Kringles, and by some seemingly cruel turn of cardiac fate it was Christmas morning and he was in the process of dying.[2] In my self-pity it did not seem right to me, and I confess I was muttering something of that aloud as I walked what surely must have been every square inch of the public (and a fair portion of the private) space in that hospital.

hen and there—2:00 or 3:00 A.M. in a very quiet hospital, immersed as I was in some sorrow and too much selfishness—heaven sent me a small, personal, prepackaged revelation, a tiny Christmas declaration that was as powerful as any I have ever received. In the midst of mumbling about the very

poor calendaring in all of this, I heard the clear, unbroken cry of a baby. It truly startled me. I had long since ceased paying attention to where I was wandering that night, and only then did I realize I was near the maternity ward; somewhere, I suppose, near the nursery. To this day I do not know just where that baby was or how I heard it. I like to think it was a brand-new baby taking that first breath and announcing that he or she had arrived in the world, the fact of which everyone was supposed to take note.

It may have just been a baby saying it was time to eat, and wondering where that comforting cuddle from a mother was. But wherever and whoever it was, God could not have sent me a more penetrating wake-up call.

I felt a little like another who, in reply to his questions, heard the Lord declare,

"WHO IS THIS THAT DARKENETH COUNSEL BY WORDS WITHOUT KNOWLEDGE?" (JOB 38:2.)

I t was as if he were saying: "Listen, Jeffrey Roy, this is the happiest night in the whole wide world for some young couple who may otherwise be poor as church mice. Maybe this is their first baby. Maybe he or she is their own personal 'consolation in Israel,' perhaps the only consolation they have right now in what may otherwise be a difficult life. In any case they love this baby, and the baby already loves them. And think of the calendaring—born on Christmas Day! What a reminder that they have each other now and forever! Whatever happens, good times or bad, they have each other. Whatever pain may lie ahead, whatever sword might pierce their souls from time to time, they will be triumphant because the Prince of Peace was also born this same day 'once in royal David's city.'

"Temporary separation at death and the other difficulties that attend us as we all move toward that end are part of the price we pay for love in this world, the price we pay for the joy of birth and family ties and the fun of Christmas together. Old Simeon, weathered and tried and tested Simeon, had it right. And so did the morning stars and the shepherds and the angels who shouted for joy, praising God and singing, 'Glory to God in the highest, and on earth peace, good will toward men.'

"Jeff, my boy," my Father in Heaven seemed to say with that baby's cry, "I expected a little more from you. If you can't remember why all of this matters, then your approach to Christmas is no more virtuous than the overcommercialization everyone laments these days. You need to shape up just a little, to put your theology where your Christmas carols are. You can't separate Bethlehem from Gethsemane or the hasty flight into Egypt from the slow journey to the summit of Calvary. It's of one piece. It is a single plan. It considers 'the fall and rising again of many in Israel,' but always in that order. Christmas is joyful not because it is a season or decade or lifetime without pain and privation, but precisely because life does hold those moments for us. And that baby, my son,

You can't separate Bethlehem
from Gethsemane or the hasty flight
into Egypt from the slow journey
to the summit of Calvary.

my own beloved and Only Begotten Son in the flesh, born 'away in a manger, [with] no crib for his bed,' makes all the difference in the world, all the difference in time and eternity, all the difference everywhere, worlds without number, a lot farther than your eye can see."

can't fully describe to you what happened to me that early yuletide morning, but it was one of the most revelatory Christmas experiences I have ever had. And it dawned on me that that could have been my young parents who were so happy that morning. I was a December baby, and my mother never wearied of telling me that that was her happiest Christmas ever.

Perhaps the joy they felt that day at my birth was to be inextricably, inseparably, eternally linked with my sorrow at their passing—that we could never expect to have the one without the other. It came to me in a profound way that in this life no one can have real love without eventually dealing with real loss, and we certainly can't rejoice over one's birth and the joy of living unless we are prepared to understand and accommodate and accept with some grace the inevitability—including the untimeliness—of difficulty and trouble and death. These are God's gifts to us—birth and life and death and salvation, the whole divine experience in all its richness and complexity.

So there lay my dad, the great gift-giver, he who found bicycles and BB guns and presents of every kind somewhere. Now he was starting to make his way out of the world on Christmas Day, on the wings of the greatest gift ever given. I thought of another Father.

> FOR GOD SO LOVED THE WORLD, THAT HE GAVE HIS ONLY BEGOTTEN SON, THAT WHOSOEVER BELIEVETH IN HIM SHOULD NOT PERISH, BUT HAVE EVERLASTING LIFE. (JOHN 3:16.)

rue fathers and mothers were all alike, I realized; coming up with the best gifts imaginable at what is often terrible personal cost—and I am obviously not speaking of material gifts or monetary costs.

So I was mildly but firmly rebuked that night—by the cry of a newborn baby. I got a little refresher course in the plan of salvation and a powerful reminder of why this is "the season to be jolly," and why any Christmas is a time of comfort, whatever our circumstances may be. In the same breath I was also reminded that life will not always be as cozy as "chestnuts roasting on an open fire" or an unending splendor while we stroll, "walking in a winter wonderland." No, life will have its valleys and peaks, its moments for the fall and rising in the lives of all of God's children. So now it is old Simeon's joyful embrace of that little baby just before his own death that is one of the images I try to remember at Christmas.

have repented since that night. In fact, I did some repenting there in the maternity ward. If you have to lose your dad, what more comforting time than the Christmas season? None of us would want those experiences for the Wilberg Mine families or the Moab seminary students or a thousand other painful experiences some people have at Christmas; but even so, in the end it is all right. It is okay. These are sad experiences, terribly wrenching experiences, with difficult moments for years and years to come. But because of the birth in Bethlehem and what it led to they are not tragic experiences. They have a happy ending. There is a rising after the falling. There is life always. New births and rebirths and resurrection to eternal life. It is the joy of the stable—the maternity ward—forever.

"If thou hadst been here, my brother had not died," (JOHN 11:21) Martha said to him once, probably in the same tone of voice I had been using up and down the hallways of the hospital. "If that arthritis

just had not required surgery, there wouldn't have
been any strain on his heart. If that conveyer belt
had just been shifted a little, it wouldn't have started
that fire. If there just hadn't been a small patch of ice
on that particular stretch of road so close to the
Colorado River. . . ." And on and on and on. Jesus
has one answer for us all—one answer to all the
"whys" and "what ifs," all the "would haves" and
"could haves" and "should haves" of our journey.

ooking sweet Martha firmly in the
eyes, he said for all in Salt Lake City
and Orangeville and Moab to hear:

I AM THE RESURRECTION, AND THE LIFE:
HE THAT BELIEVETH IN ME, THOUGH HE WERE
DEAD, YET SHALL HE LIVE:
    AND WHOSOEVER LIVETH AND BELIEVETH
IN ME SHALL NEVER DIE. (JOHN 11:25–26.)

Yes, for me the most important Christmas visitor
of all may have been old Simeon, who, not in the

75

absence of hard days and long years but because of them, would sing with us tonight at the top of his voice, "Joy to the world, the Lord is come; let earth receive her King! . . . No more will sin and sorrow grow, nor thorns infest the ground; he'll come and make the blessings flow, far as the curse was found."[3] Of this witness I am a witness. In the name of Jesus Christ, amen.

NOTES

1. "I HEARD THE BELLS ON CHRISTMAS DAY," HYMNS, NO. 214.
2. AFTER SEVERAL DAYS OF SLIPPING IN AND OUT OF CONSCIOUSNESS, MY FATHER PASSED AWAY SHORTLY INTO THE NEW YEAR.
3. "JOY TO THE WORLD," HYMNS, NO. 201.